The Sorrowful Mysteries

The Sorrowful Mysteries
Copyright © 2023
Sara Swann

ISBN: 978-1-957344-88-1

Cover design by Mike Parker

Published by WordCrafts Press
Cody, Wyoming 82414
www.wordcrafts.net

The Sorrowful Mysteries

Mysteries of the Rosary for Children
Volume 2

SARA SWANN

WordCrafts Press

It is only fitting that this volume be dedicated to my child with a humble, holy heart and a lovely devotion to the Rosary—my firstborn son, Logan. God has great things in store for you, and I'm blessed to be your mother!
I love you to the moon and back!

Getting Started

The first step in praying your Rosary is to get ready. For each mystery below, the prayers you pray will be written in **bold**, so you know what to say, just like the responses you say in Mass, and their Latin translations are there in ***bold italics***, too.

Now, look at your Rosary. Every Rosary has a crucifix, a medallion, six big beads, and 53 smaller beads. All these beads help us pray lots of prayers, and that is just one of the many reasons that make the Rosary so special.

You might be asking, what prayers go where? There are only seven prayers you need to know to pray the Rosary.

1. The Sign of the Cross
2. The Apostles' Creed
3. The Hail Mary
4. The Glory Be
5. The Fatima Prayer
6. The Hail Holy Queen
7. The Final Prayer.

The Sign of the Cross always bookends, or begins and ends, the Rosary just as it begins and ends all our prayers.

The Crucifix is for the Apostle's Creed. The big beads are for the Our Father prayer, and the small beads are for the Hail Mary. The other prayers are sprinkled throughout.

Did you know . . .
We pray these mysteries on Mondays, Saturdays, and during Advent and Christmas season Sundays, too.

Are you ready to get started?
Let's go!

TUESDAYS AND FRIDAYS
(And Sundays during Lent)

The Sorrowful Mysteries

uring these Sorrowful Mysteries, you will walk with Jesus through His Passion and Crucifixion. Begin with your Rosary in your hand.

Do the Sign of the Cross by touching your Rosary to your forehead, then your chest, then left shoulder, then your right shoulder.

You can remember this because God the Father is in Heaven above us (touch your forehead), God the Son lives in your heart (touch your chest), and Jesus carried the Cross on His shoulders (touch your left shoulder then your right shoulder). When you say amen, put your hands together in front of you, like prayer hands.

> **In the name of the Father,**
>> *In nomine Patris,*
>>> *(Forehead)*
>
> **and of the Son,**
>> *et Filii,*
>>> *(Chest or Heart)*
>
> **and of the Holy Spirit.**
>> *Et Spiritus Sancti.*
>>> *(Left then Right Shoulder)*

Amen.

> *Amen.*
> *(End with prayer hands)*

Now you are ready to begin praying your Rosary. First, hold the Crucifix and pray the Apostles' Creed.

I believe in God,

> *Credo in Deum*

the Father almighty,

> *Patrem omnipoténtem,*

Creator of heaven and earth,

> *Creatórem cæli et terræ.*

And in Jesus Christ,

> *Et in Iesum Christum,*

His only Son,

> *Fílium eius únicum,*

Our Lord,

> *Dóminum nostrum,*

Who was conceived by the Holy Spirit,

> *qui concéptus est de Spíritu Sancto,*

Born of the Virgin Mary,

> *natus ex María Vírgine,*

Suffered under Pontius Pilate,

> *passus sub Póntio Piláto,*

Was crucified, died, and was buried;

> *crucifíxus, mórtuus, et sepúltus,*

He descended into hell;

> *descéndit ad ínfernos,*

On the third day;

> *tértia die;*

He rose again from the dead;

> *resurréxit a mórtuis;*

He ascended into Heaven,

ascéndit ad cælos,

And is seated at the right hand of God,

sedet ad déxteram Dei,

The Father Almighty,

Patris omnipoténtis,

And from there He will come

inde ventúrus

to judge the living and the dead.

est iudicáre vivos et mórtuos.

I believe in the Holy Spirit,

Credo in Spíritum Sanctum,

The Holy Catholic Church,

sanctam Ecclésiam cathólicam,

The communion of Saints,

sanctórum communiónem,

The forgiveness of sins,

remissiónem peccatórum,

The resurrection of the body,

carnis resurrectiónem,

And life everlasting.

vitam ætérnam.

Amen.

Amen.

Now, move your fingers up to the next bead. It is bigger than the other beads and may even be a different color, so you know this bead is for the Our Father prayer.

Our Father, who art in heaven,

Pater noster, qui es in cælis,

hallowed be Thy name.

sanctificétur nomen tuum.

Thy kingdom come,

Advéniat regnum tuum.

Thy will be done,

Fiat volúntas tua,

On earth as it is in heaven.

sicut in cælo, et in terra.

And give us this day our daily bread,

Panem nostrum quotidiánum da nobis hódie,

And forgive us our trespasses,

et dimítte nobis débita nostra sicut

As we forgive those who trespass against us,

et nos dimíttimus debitóribus nostris.

And lead us not into temptation,

Et ne nos indúcas in tentatiónem,

But deliver us from evil.

sed líbera nos a malo.

Amen.

Amen.

Next, we have three small beads. You already know these are for the Hail Mary prayers. Each one of these three beads are special for a different reason. These special beads help open our hearts to be more like Mother Mary in our own *Faith*, *Hope*, and *Charity*.

Did you know . . .
Another word for charity is love.

Move your fingers to the first Hail Mary bead. This Hail Mary bead is the *Faith* bead. We ask for an increase in our Faith as we pray the Hail Mary prayer.

Hail Mary, full of grace,

Ave María, grátia plena,

the Lord is with thee.

Dóminus tecum.

Blessed art thou amongst women,

Benedícta tu in muliéribus,

and blessed is the fruit of thy womb, Jesus.

et benedíctus fructus ventris tui, Iesus.

Holy Mary, Mother of God,

Sancta María, Mater Dei,

Pray for us sinners,

ora pro nobis peccatóribus,

Now and at the hour of our death.

nunc, et in hora mortis nostræ.

Amen.

Amen.

Now, move your fingers to the second small bead. On this bead, we pray the Hail Mary prayer and ask for an increase in our *Hope*.

Hail Mary, full of grace,

Ave María, grátia plena,

the Lord is with thee.

Dóminus tecum.

Blessed art thou amongst women,

Benedícta tu in muliéribus,

and blessed is the fruit of thy womb, Jesus.

et benedíctus fructus ventris tui, Iesus.

Holy Mary, Mother of God,

Sancta María, Mater Dei,

Pray for us sinners,

ora pro nobis peccatóribus,

Now and at the hour of our death.

> *nunc, et in hora mortis nostræ.*

Amen.

> *Amen.*

Finally, move your fingers to the third small bead. On this bead, we pray the Hail Mary prayer and ask for an increase in our *Charity* or *Love*.

Hail Mary, full of grace,

> *Ave María, grátia plena,*

the Lord is with thee.

> *Dóminus tecum.*

Blessed art thou amongst women,

> *Benedícta tu in muliéribus,*

and blessed is the fruit of thy womb, Jesus.

> *et benedíctus fructus ventris tui, Iesus.*

Holy Mary, Mother of God,

> *Sancta María, Mater Dei,*

Pray for us sinners,

> *ora pro nobis peccatóribus,*

Now and at the hour of our death.

> *nunc, et in hora mortis nostræ.*

Amen.

> *Amen.*

Remember those surprise prayers we talked about earlier? Here is the first time you find them in the Rosary!

With your fingers still on the bead, you say two very special prayers. First, is the Glory Be. When you say the Glory Be prayer, you bow to the Crucifix to show respect and love to Jesus Christ. Then, you say the Fatima Prayer. Sometimes, the Fatima Prayer is sometimes called the O My Jesus prayer.

Did you remember . . .
to bow to your crucifix whenever
you pray a Glory Be?

Glory Be

                                        Glória

to the Father,

                                        Patri,

and to the Son,

                                        et Fílio,

and to the Holy Spirit.

                                et Spirítui Sancto.

As it was in the beginning,

                                Sicut erat in princípio,

Is now,

                                        et nunc,

And ever shall be,

                                        et semper,

World without end.

                                et in sæcula sæculórum.

Amen.

                                        Amen.

Then, pray your Fatima Prayer.

O My Jesus,

                                Dómine Jesu,

Forgive us our sins,

                                dimitte nobis débita nostra,

And save us from the fires of hell.

                                salva nos ab igne inferni,

Lead all souls to heaven,

perduc in caelum omnes ánimas,

Especially those in most need of thy

praesertim eas, quae misericórdiae tuae

mercy.

máxime indigent.

Now you're ready to begin your first Sorrowful Mystery!

The First Sorrowful Mystery

The Agony in the Garden

The First Joyful Mystery comes from the Gospel of St. Matthew. The Scripture for the first Sorrowful Mystery tells us why this mystery is important.

"Then Jesus went with them to a place called Gethsemane, and he said to his disciples, 'Sit here, while I go yonder and pray.'

And taking with him Peter and the two sons of Zebedee, he began to be sorrowful and troubled.

Then he said to them, 'My soul is very sorrowful, even to death; remain here, and watch with me.'

And going a little farther he fell on his face and prayed, 'My Father, if it be possible, let this cup pass from me; nevertheless, not as I will, but as you will.'"

St. Matthew 26:36–39

Activity . . .
Find the Garden of Gethsemane on a map.

Move up to the next big bead. Remember, this is an Our Father bead.

Our Father, who art in heaven,

Pater noster, qui es in cælis,

hallowed be Thy name.

sanctificétur nomen tuum.

Thy kingdom come,

Advéniat regnum tuum.

Thy will be done,

Fiat volúntas tua,

On earth as it is in heaven.

sicut in cælo, et in terra.

And give us this day our daily bread,

Panem nostrum quotidiánum da nobis hódie,

And forgive us our trespasses,

> *et dimítte nobis débita nostra sicut*

As we forgive those who trespass against us,

> *et nos dimíttimus debitóribus nostris.*

And lead us not into temptation,

> *Et ne nos indúcas in tentatiónem,*

But deliver us from evil.

> *sed líbera nos a malo.*

Amen.

> *Amen.*

Next, pray ten Hail Mary prayers while you think about the Scripture.

Pro Tip . . .

The Sorrowful Mysteries are sad, and they can make us sad, too. It is important to remember that Jesus went through these things willingly because He loves us so much and wants us to spend eternity with Him in Heaven.

Hail Mary, full of grace,

> *Ave María, grátia plena,*

the Lord is with thee.

> *Dóminus tecum.*

Blessed art thou amongst women,

> *Benedícta tu in muliéribus,*

and blessed is the fruit of thy womb, Jesus.

> *et benedíctus fructus ventris tui, Iesus.*

Holy Mary, Mother of God,

> *Sancta María, Mater Dei,*

Pray for us sinners,

ora pro nobis peccatóribus,

Now and at the hour of our death.

nunc, et in hora mortis nostræ.

Amen.

Amen.

Remember the two special prayers, The Glory Be and The Fatima Prayer, that are hidden throughout our Rosary? You just found them again! Keep holding the tenth bead and pray a Glory Be and a Fatima Prayer. Remember to bow to your Crucifix when you pray your Glory Be.

Glory Be

Glória

to the Father,

Patri,

and to the Son,

et Fílio,

and to the Holy Spirit.

et Spirítui Sancto.

As it was in the beginning,

Sicut erat in princípio,

Is now,

et nunc,

And ever shall be,

et semper,

World without end.

et in sæcula sæculórum.

Amen.

Amen.

Then, pray your Fatima Prayer.

O My Jesus,

Dómine Jesu,

Forgive us our sins,

dimitte nobis débita nostra,

And save us from the fires of hell.

salva nos ab igne inferni,

Lead all souls to heaven,

perduc in caelum omnes ánimas,

Especially those in most need of thy

praesertim eas, quae misericórdiae tuae

mercy.

máxime indigent.

Thoughts to Consider . . .
Remember, mysteries tell the story of Jesus's betrayal and death on the cross.

Congratulations! You have just finished praying your first decade of the Sorrowful Mysteries Rosary!

As you prayed, you thought about how Jesus did God's Will and accepted it even when it was scary. Jesus had complete faith and trust in God, and He knew that no matter what, God's will was the most important thing of all. Write down some of your thoughts on the next page.

The Second Sorrowful Mystery

The Scourging at the Pillar

T he Second Sorrowful Mystery, like the first, also comes from the Book of St. Matthew and tells us why this mystery is important.

Pilate released Barabbas to them, but after he had Jesus scourged, he handed him over to be crucified.

St. Matthew 27, 26

Did you know . . .

The fruit of this mystery is purity. We can show Jesus how much we love Him and appreciate how He sacrificed His body for us by remembering that our flesh is sacred, too.

Move your fingers to the next big, Our Father bead.

Our Father, who art in heaven,

Pater noster, qui es in cælis,

hallowed be Thy name.

sanctificétur nomen tuum.

Thy kingdom come,

Advéniat regnum tuum.

Thy will be done,

Fiat volúntas tua,

On earth as it is in heaven.

sicut in cælo, et in terra.

And give us this day our daily bread,

Panem nostrum quotidiánum da nobis hódie,

And forgive us our trespasses,

et dimítte nobis débita nostra sicut

As we forgive those who trespass against us,

et nos dimíttimus debitóribus nostris.

And lead us not into temptation,

Et ne nos indúcas in tentatiónem,

But deliver us from evil.

sed líbera nos a malo.

Amen.

Amen.

Move your fingers along the beads as you pray ten Hail Mary prayers and think about the Scripture. Also think about how much Jesus loves you to have gone through his Passion willingly.

Hail Mary, full of grace,

Ave María, grátia plena,

the Lord is with thee.

Dóminus tecum.

Blessed art thou amongst women,

Benedícta tu in muliéribus,

and blessed is the fruit of thy womb, Jesus.

et benedíctus fructus ventris tui, Iesus.

Holy Mary, Mother of God,

Sancta María, Mater Dei,

Pray for us sinners,

ora pro nobis peccatóribus,

Now and at the hour of our death.

nunc, et in hora mortis nostræ.

Amen.

Amen.

> **Did you know . . .**
> All the mysteries of the Rosary are taken from Scripture.

Keep holding the tenth bead and pray a Glory Be and a Fatima Prayer. Remember to bow to your crucifix when you pray your Glory Be.

Glory Be

Glória

to the Father,

Patri,

and to the Son,

et Fílio,

and to the Holy Spirit.

et Spirítui Sancto.

As it was in the beginning,

Sicut erat in princípio,

Is now,

et nunc,

And ever shall be,

et semper,

World without end.

et in sæcula sæculórum.

Amen.

Amen.

Then, pray your Fatima Prayer.

O My Jesus,

Dómine Jesu,

Forgive us our sins,

dimitte nobis débita nostra,

And save us from the fires of hell.

salva nos ab igne inferni,

Lead all souls to heaven,

perduc in caelum omnes ánimas,

Especially those in most need of thy

praesertim eas, quae misericórdiae tuae

mercy.

máxime indigent.

Did you know . . .

Jesus felt every sin from all of humanity during the night of His Passion—that includes all of your sins and all of my sins, too.

How about that! You have just finished praying your second decade of the Rosary!

As you prayed, you thought about how you can live your life to honor Jesus. What do you think are some ways you can live your life to honor Jesus and the sacrifice He made for you? Write down some of your thoughts on the next page.

The Third Sorrowful Mystery

The Crowning with Thorns

The Third Sorrowful Mystery comes from the Gospel of St. Matthew.

Did you know . . .
The wounds Jesus suffered are visible on the
Shroud of Turin.

*Then the soldiers of the governor took Jesus into the
praetorium, and they gathered the whole battalion before
him.*

*And they stripped him and put a scarlet robe upon
him, and plaiting a crown of thorns, they put it on his
head, and put a reed in his right hand.*

*And kneeling before him they mocked him, saying,
'Hail, King of the Jews!'*

St. Matthew 27:27–29

Move your fingers to the next big, Our Father bead.

Our Father, who art in heaven,

Pater noster, qui es in cælis,

hallowed be Thy name.

sanctificétur nomen tuum.

Thy kingdom come,

Advéniat regnum tuum.

Thy will be done,

Fiat volúntas tua,

On earth as it is in heaven.

sicut in cælo, et in terra.

And give us this day our daily bread,

Panem nostrum quotidiánum da nobis hódie,

And forgive us our trespasses,

dimítte nobis débita nostra sicut

As we forgive those who trespass against us,
> *et nos dimíttimus debitóribus nostris.*

And lead us not into temptation,
> *Et ne nos indúcas in tentatiónem,*

But deliver us from evil.
> *sed líbera nos a malo.*

Amen.
> *Amen.*

Move your fingers along the beads as you pray ten Hail Mary prayers and think about the Scripture. Also think about ways you can show Jesus's love to others.

Thoughts to Consider . . .

The fruit of this mystery is letting Jesus reign as the king of your heart. We know that Jesus's kingdom is in Heaven. So how can we show His love here on earth?

Hail Mary, full of grace,
> *Ave María, grátia plena,*

the Lord is with thee.
> *Dóminus tecum.*

Blessed art thou amongst women,
> *Benedícta tu in muliéribus,*

and blessed is the fruit of thy womb, Jesus.
> *et benedíctus fructus ventris tui, Iesus.*

Holy Mary, Mother of God,
> *Sancta María, Mater Dei,*

Pray for us sinners,
> *ora pro nobis peccatóribus,*

Now and at the hour of our death.

nunc, et in hora mortis nostræ.

Amen.

Amen.

Keep holding the tenth bead and pray a Glory Be and a Fatima Prayer. Remember to bow to your crucifix when you pray your Glory Be.

Glory Be

Glória

to the Father,

Patri,

and to the Son,

et Fílio,

and to the Holy Spirit.

et Spirítui Sancto.

As it was in the beginning,

Sicut erat in princípio,

Is now,

et nunc,

And ever shall be,

et semper,

World without end.

et in sæcula sæculórum.

Amen.

Amen.

Did you know . . .
Mother Mary's first apparition in Fatima, Portugal was May 13, 1917, during World War I?.

Now, it's time for the Fatima Prayer.

O My Jesus,
> *Dómine Jesu,*

Forgive us our sins,
> *dimitte nobis débita nostra,*

And save us from the fires of hell.
> *salva nos ab igne inferni.*

Lead all souls to heaven,
> *perduc in caelum omnes ánimas,*

Especially those in most need of thy
> *praesertim eas, quae misericórdiae tuae*

mercy.
> *máxime indigent.*

Great job! You have just finished praying your third decade of the Rosary!

Thoughs to Consider . . .
When Mother Mary appeared to the three shepherd children, she told them two things could bring an end to World War I; praying the Rosary and offering up suffering.

As you prayed, you thought about how Jesus was mocked, ridiculed, and crowned with thorns. What are some ways you can keep Jesus as the king of your heart? Write down some of your ideas on the next page

The Fourth Sorrowful Mystery

The Carrying of the Cross

The Fourth Sorrowful Mystery comes from the Gospel of St. Mark

And they compelled a passer-by, Simon of Cyrene, who was coming in from the country, the father of Alexander and Rufus, to carry his cross.

And they brought him to the place called Golgotha (which means the place of a skull).

St. Mark 15:21-22

Did you know . . .

St. Simon of Cyrene did not want to help Jesus carry the cross, but he did anyway. The fruit of this mystery is obedience.

Move your fingers to the next big, Our Father bead.

Our Father, who art in heaven,

Pater noster, qui es in cælis,

hallowed be Thy name.

sanctificétur nomen tuum.

Thy kingdom come,

Advéniat regnum tuum.

Thy will be done,

Fiat volúntas tua,

On earth as it is in heaven.

sicut in cælo, et in terra.

And give us this day our daily bread,

Panem nostrum quotidiánum da nobis hódie,

And forgive us our trespasses,

et dimítte nobis débita nostra sicut

As we forgive those who trespass against us,

et nos dimíttimus debitóribus nostris.

And lead us not into temptation,

Et ne nos indúcas in tentatiónem,

30

But deliver us from evil.

sed líbera nos a malo.

Amen.

Amen.

Move your fingers along the beads as you pray ten Hail Mary prayers and think about the Scripture. Also think about ways you can show obedience in your life.

Did you know . . .

Many Saints came about during Jesus's Passion. St. Simon and St. Veronica were there on the path to Golgotha as Jesus carried the cross.

Hail Mary, full of grace,

Ave María, grátia plena,

the Lord is with thee.

Dóminus tecum.

Blessed art thou amongst women,

Benedícta tu in muliéribus,

and blessed is the fruit of thy womb, Jesus.

et benedíctus fructus ventris tui, Iesus.

Holy Mary, Mother of God,

Sancta María, Mater Dei,

Pray for us sinners,

ora pro nobis peccatóribus,

Now and at the hour of our death.

nunc, et in hora mortis nostræ.

Amen.

Amen.

Keep holding the tenth bead and pray a Glory Be and a Fatima Prayer. Remember to bow to your crucifix when you pray your Glory Be.

Glory Be

Glória

to the Father,

Patri,

and to the Son,

et Fílio,

and to the Holy Spirit.

et Spirítui Sancto.

As it was in the beginning,

Sicut erat in princípio,

Is now,

et nunc,

And ever shall be,

et semper,

World without end.

et in sæcula sæculórum.

Amen.

Amen.

Now, it's time for the Fatima Prayer.

O My Jesus,

Dómine Jesu,

Forgive us our sins,

dimitte nobis débita nostra,

And save us from the fires of hell.

salva nos ab igne inferni,

Lead all souls to heaven,

perduc in caelum omnes ánimas,

Especially those in most need of thy

praesertim eas, quae misericórdiae tuae

mercy.

máxime indigent.

Look how far you've come! You have just finished praying your fourth decade of the Rosary!

As you prayed, you thought about how St. Simon of Cyrene was obedient and helped Jesus, even when he did not want to. What do you think are some way you can be obedient, like St. Simon when he helped Jesus in his time of need. Write down some of your thoughts on the next page.

The Fifth Sorrowful Mystery

The Crucifixion

The Fifth Sorrowful Mystery comes from the Gospel of St. Luke.

And when they came to the place which is called The Skull, there they crucified him, and the criminals, one on the right and one on the left.

And Jesus said, 'Father, forgive them; for they know not what they do' ...

It was now about the sixth hour, and there was darkness over the whole land until the ninth hour, while the sun's light failed; and the curtain of the temple was torn in two.

Then Jesus, crying with a loud voice, said, 'Father, into thy hands I commit my spirit!'

And having said this, he breathed his last.

St. Luke 23:33–46

Thoughts to Consider . . .

The fruit of this mystery is pardoning, or for-giving, those who have injured us.

Move your fingers to the next big, Our Father bead.

Our Father, who art in heaven,

Pater noster, qui es in cælis,

hallowed be Thy name.

sanctificétur nomen tuum.

Thy kingdom come,

Advéniat regnum tuum.

Thy will be done,

Fiat volúntas tua,

On earth as it is in heaven.

sicut in cælo, et in terra.

And give us this day our daily bread,

Panem nostrum quotidiánum da nobis hódie,

And forgive us our trespasses,

et dimítte nobis débita nostra sicut

As we forgive those who trespass against us,

et nos dimíttimus debitóribus nostris.

And lead us not into temptation,

Et ne nos indúcas in tentatiónem,

But deliver us from evil.

sed líbera nos a malo.

Amen.

Amen.

Did you know . . .

The mysteries of this Sorrowful Mystery came from the Gospels of St. Matthew, St. Mark, and St. Luke.

Move your fingers along the beads as you pray ten Hail Mary prayers and think about the Scripture. Think about how Jesus asked God to forgive the people who tortured him and put him to death on the cross.

Hail Mary, full of grace,

Ave María, grátia plena,

the Lord is with thee.

Dóminus tecum.

Blessed art thou amongst women,

Benedícta tu in muliéribus,

and blessed is the fruit of thy womb, Jesus.

et benedíctus fructus ventris tui, Iesus.

Holy Mary, Mother of God,

Sancta María, Mater Dei,

Pray for us sinners,

ora pro nobis peccatóribus,

Now and at the hour of our death.

nunc, et in hora mortis nostræ.

Amen.

Amen.

Keep holding the tenth bead and pray a Glory Be and a Fatima Prayer. Remember to bow to your crucifix when you pray your Glory Be.

Glory Be

Glória

to the Father,

Patri,

and to the Son,

et Fílio,

and to the Holy Spirit.

et Spirítui Sancto.

As it was in the beginning,

Sicut erat in princípio,

Is now,

et nunc,

And ever shall be,

et semper,

World without end.

et in sæcula sæculórum.

Amen.

Amen.

Now, it's time for the Fatima Prayer.

O My Jesus,

Dómine Jesu,

Forgive us our sins,

dimitte nobis débita nostra,

And save us from the fires of hell.

salva nos ab igne inferni,

Lead all souls to heaven,

perduc in caelum omnes ánimas,

Especially those in most need of thy

praesertim eas, quae misericórdiae tuae

mercy.

máxime indigent.

You're almost finished praying your the entire Sorrowful Mysteries of the Rosary!

As you prayed, you thought about how much Jesus loves all of us, even those who hurt him. How do you think it must have felt to see Jesus forgive the people who hurt him. Does it make you feel like you can forgive all kinds of people in your life, too? On the next page, write down some of your thoughts about how the people present at the Crucifixion must have felt when Jesus forgave his captors.

The Mystery of the Rosary

The Ending of Each Mystery

The ending of each Mystery of the Rosary consists of two very special prayers: The Hail Holy Queen and The Final Prayer.

Hail Holy Queen

Hail Holy Queen,

Salve Regína,

Mother of Mercy,

mater misericórdiæ;

our Life, our Sweetness, and our hope.

vita, dulcédo, et spes nostra, salve.

To thee we cry,

Ad te Clamámus

poor banished children of Eve.

éxsules fílii Evæ;

To thee we send up our sighs,

Ad te Suspirámus,

mourning and weeping in this valley of tears.

geméntes et flentes in hac lacrimárum valle.

Turn then most gracious advocate,

Eia ergo, Advocáta nostra,

Thine eyes of mercy toward us,

Illos tuos misericórdes óculos ad nos convérte:

and after this, our exile,

Et Iesum, benedíctum fructum

show unto us,

ventris tui, Nobis post hoc exsílium

the blessed fruit of thy womb, Jesus.

osténde.

O clement, O loving, O sweet Virgin Mary.

O clemens, o pia, o dulcis Virgo María.

Pray for us O Holy Mother of God,

Ora pro nobis, Sancta Dei Genetrix.

that we may be made worthy

Ut digni efficiamur

of the promises of Christ.

promissiónibus Christi.

Amen.

Amen.

The Final Prayer ends each Mystery of the Rosary.

Let us pray.

Oremus.

O God, whose only begotten Son,

Déus, cújus Unigénitus

by His life, death, and resurrection,

per vítam, mortem, et resurrectiónem

has purchased for us the

Súam nóbis salútis

rewards of eternal life,

ætérnæ præmia comparávit:

grant, we beseech Thee,

concéde, quæsumus:

that meditating upon these mysteries

ut hæc mystéria

of the Most Holy Rosary of

sacratíssimo beátæ

the Blessed Virgin Mary,

Maríæ Vírginis Rosário recoléntes,

we may imitate what they contain

et imitémur quod cóntinent,

and obtain what they promise,

et quod promíttunt, assequámur.

through the same Christ Our Lord.

Per eúndem Chrístum Dóminum nóstrum.

Amen.

Amen.

Remember what bookends all your prayers—including your Rosary prayers—The Sign of the Cross.

In the name of the Father,

In nomine Patris,

(Forehead)

and of the Son,

et Filii,

(Chest or Heart)

and of the Holy Spirit.

Et Spiritus Sancti.

(Left then Right Shoulder)

Amen.

Amen.

(End with prayer hands)

Acknowledgements

There are so many I would like to thank for helping the Mysteries of the Rosary for Children series come to fruition. My children, who not only stood by me as I taught myself to draw and then to paint in order to create the illustrations for this series, but drew and painted right along with me. My parents, who not only encouraged this project from the beginning, but were just as excited as me as each painting progressed and came to *life*. To my publishers, Mike and Paula, as they championed this project from the beginning, deep within the throes of the pandemic.

> *And the angel said to them: Fear not; for, behold, I bring you good tidings of great joy that shall be to all the people. For today, a Savior has been born for you in the city of David: he is Christ the Lord. And this will be a sign for you: you will find the infant wrapped in swaddling clothes and lying in a manger. And suddenly there was with the Angel a multitude of the celestial army, praising God and saying, Glory to God in the highest, and on earth peace to men of good will.*
>
> St. Luke 2:10–14 NIV

Sara Swann-Barnard BSN, RN

ABOUT THE AUTHOR

Sara Swann loves to write and has more than thirty credited works available in print.

She holds a Bachelor of Arts degree in History and spent several years as a teacher in West Texas before earning a Bachelor of Science degree in Nursing. She now works as an emergency room nurse in Houston, Texas, where she, her children, and their menagerie of rescue pets—six in all—make their home.

In her spare time, Sara and her family enjoy ice cream and the beach, but she wishes someone who majored in Physics and Engineering would hurry up and invent a time machine so she could meet St. Francis of Assisi, Henry VIII, William Wallace, and Vlad the Impaler.

Connect with Sara online at:

www.NurseSaraBooks.com